Football
Wit

summersdale

Summersdale Publishers Ltd
46 West Street
Chichester
West Sussex
PO19 1RP
UK

www.summersdale.com

Printed and bound in Great Britain

ISBN: 978-1-84024-671-1

Disclaimer
Every effort has been made to attribute the quotations in
this collection to the correct source. Should there be any
omissions or errors in this respect we apologise and shall
be pleased to make the appropriate acknowledgements in
any future editions.

Football
Wit

Aubrey Malone

Contents

Editor's Note

Football players aren't necessarily expected to be funny, or even articulate. As Brian Clough once noted, their brains are in their feet. Which means that when someone comes out with a thought-provoking comment, like for instance Eric Cantona's famous pronouncement on press intrusiveness ('When the seagulls follow the trawler, it is because they think sardines will be thrown into the sea'), people react almost as if they've just heard a latter-day Shakespeare.

A lot of the so-called wit in these pages is unwitting, if you'll forgive the contradiction. This is the football world's confused (and often confusing) meanderings on lame duck managers, overpriced (and under-performing) stars, visually challenged referees and cash-hungry magnates.

If you're an aficionado of *Match of the Day* you'll know what it's like to suffer dull post mortems. But occasionally a pundit comes out with a nugget – intentionally or otherwise – and it's up to anthologists like me to commit these to memory and regurgitate them for your delectation.

As the man said, football's a funny old game.

CAN YOU MANAGE IT?

There's only one
certainty in football:
managers get sacked.

Brian Kerr

Steve McClaren has achieved the unique feat of making even Sven Goran-Eriksson look good.

Ian Ridley

There are two types of manager: those who've just been sacked and those who are just about to be.

Howard Wilkinson

Barry Fry's management is based on the chaos theory.

Mark McGhee

—•—

For me to win the Manager of the Month award I would have to win nine games out of eight.

Sheffield United's Neil Warnock in 2003

—•—

You're not a real manager until you've been sacked.

Malcolm Allison

Even Ferguson and Wenger
had their recurrent weaknesses;
neither, to take a common instance,
appeared capable of distinguishing
a top-class goalkeeper from a
cheese-and-tomato sandwich.

Patrick Barclay

Alex Ferguson is the best manager
I've had at this level. Well, he's the
only manager I've had at this level.

David Beckham

Arsene Wenger and Alex Ferguson don't conduct post-match pleasantries as a general rule. The Arsenal manager would, however, be happy to crack open a bottle of red with his Manchester United counterpart – provided he could use the Scot's head as a corkscrew.

Andrew Fifield

If a manager isn't fired with enthusiasm he'll be fired – with enthusiasm.

Joe Lovejoy

The easiest team for a manager
to pick is the Hindsight Eleven.

Craig Brown

❦

A manager must buy cheap and
sell dear. If another manager rings
to ask me about a player I'll say
'He's great, super lad, goes to
church twice a day. Good in the
air, two lovely feet, make a great
son-in-law.' You never tell them he
couldn't trap a bag of cement.

Tommy Docherty

Chelsea have just launched a new aftershave called 'The Special One' by U Go Boss.

Pat Flanagan after Jose Mourinho's shock departure from Chelsea in September 2007

***

Anyone who's thinking of applying for the job of Scotland manager in the next eight or nine years should go and get themselves checked out by about 15 psychiatrists.

Martin O'Neill

The secret of being a good
manager is to keep the six
players who hate you away from
the five who are undecided.

Jock Stein

If Mickey Mouse had taken charge,
it would have given the place a lift.

Mike Walker on Everton in 1994

I have come to the conclusion
that nice men do not make
the best managers.

Graeme Souness

Matt Busby was the eternal
optimist. In 1968 he still believed
that Glenn Miller was just missing.

Patrick Crerand

Great leaders inspire their men
to glory. Steve McClaren will be
remembered as a wally with a brolly.

Daily Mail

The three greatest football
managers of all time were Jock
Stein, Jock Stein and Jock Stein.

Doug McLeod

IGNORANCE IS BLISS

When God gave
Paul Gascoigne his
enormous footballing
talent, he took his
brain out at the same
time to even things up.

Tony Banks

An oxymoron is when two contradictory concepts are juxtaposed, as in 'footballing brain'.

Patrick Murray

When I signed Jim Holton from Shrewsbury for £100,000, Harry Gregg told me I had a player who didn't know the meaning of the word defeat. I told him defeat wasn't the only word he didn't understand. There was also pass, control, dribble...

Tommy Docherty

Ponderous as a carthorse and slow-witted as a football donkey, it's hardly Vinnie Jones's fault that such a clodhopper – sorry, former hod-carrier – has been able to wrangle a prosperous living from the professional game.

Jeff Powell

He's got the brains of a rocking horse.

Dave Bassett on Sheffield United goalkeeper Simon Tracey

Jason Roberts? This is a man who spelt his name wrong on his transfer request.

Gary Megson

Slim Jim had everything
required of a great Scottish
footballer. Outrageously skilled,
totally irresponsible, supremely
arrogant and thick as mince.

**Alastair McSporran on former
Rangers player Jim Baxter**

Dan Quayle thinks the Gaza Strip
is Paul Gascoigne's football jersey.

Johnny Carson

The trouble with you, son, is that your brains are all in your head.

Bill Shankly to one of his players
who underwhelmed him

He's incredibly loyal. Ask him to jump off the stand roof and he'll do it. But he's as thick as two short planks. He always grabbed the quiz book on our coach trips so he could ask the questions. That way he didn't have to answer them.

Physiotherapist Arnie Reed on Vinnie Jones

Paul Gascoigne wore a Number 10 jersey. I thought that was his position, but it turned out it was his IQ.

George Best

———

The match will be shown on *Match of the Day* this evening. If you don't want to know the result, look away now as we show you Tony Adams lifting the trophy for Arsenal.

Steve Rider

———

Well, I can play in the centre, on the right, and occasionally on the left-hand side.

David Beckham, when asked if it would be fair to describe him as a volatile player

WHISTLE-STOP TOURS

What whistles
and licks Alex
Ferguson's arse?
A Premiership
referee.

Anon

I'm trying to be careful what I say,
but the referee was useless.

David Jones

The referee was booking so
many people I thought he was
filling in his lottery numbers.

Ian Wright

Football is a game with 22 players,
two linesmen and 20,000 referees.

Bob Monkhouse

After the match an official asked
for two of my players to take a dope
test. I offered them the referee.

Tommy Docherty

I've seen harder tackles in the pie queue at half-time than the ones punished in games.

Former Falkirk chairman George
Fulston on overly strict referees

I used to play football in my youth but then my eyes went bad so I became a referee.

Eric Morecambe

———◆———

The trouble with referees is that they just don't care which side wins.

Tom Canterbury

———◆———

I never comment on referees and I'm not going to break the habit of a lifetime for that prat.

Ron Atkinson

Can anyone tell me why they give referees a watch? It certainly isn't to keep the time.

Alex Ferguson

If the fourth official had done his job it wouldn't have happened, but I don't want to blame anyone.

John Aldridge

FANNING THE FLAMES

Every fan you ask
will say he wants
to see lively, open
football, but what the
fan really wants to
see is his team win.

Dennis Hill-Wood

A real Irish football fan is one who knows the nationality of every player on the Republic of Ireland team.

Jack Charlton

McTavish: 'I hear you went over to Aberdeen to see the match last Saturday. Was it a big gate?' MacDonald: 'It was for sure. One of the biggest I've ever climbed over.'

Edward Phillips

Why do Arsenal
fans smell?
So the blind can
hate them as well.

Joe Lynam

England have the best fans in
the world, and Scotland's ones
are also second to none.

Kevin Keegan

THE SHIT HITS THE FAN

Newspaper headline after Eric Cantona's famous
attack on a Crystal Palace supporter in 1995

The fans like to see Balde
wear his shirt on his sleeve.

Kenny Dalglish

CREATIVE MATHEMATICS

I've got 14 bookings this season, 8 of which were my fault and 7 of which were disputable.

Paul Gascoigne

Argentina are the second best
team in the world, and there's
no higher praise than that.

Kevin Keegan

This will be their nineteenth
consecutive game without a win
unless they can get an equaliser.

Alan Green

Kevin Keegan and I have 63
international caps between
us. He has 63 of them.

Craig Brown

Ireland will give 99 per cent
– everything they've got.

Mark Lawrenson

Southampton have beaten
Brighton by 3 goals to 1. That's
a repeat of last year's result
when Southampton won 5–1.

Des Lynam

———

They've won 66 games, and
scored in all of them.

Brian Moore

Ritchie has now scored 11 goals, exactly double the number he got last season.

Alan Furry

—◆—

We must have had 99 per cent of the game. It was the other 3 per cent that cost us the match.

Ruud Gullit

One year I played for
fifteen months.

Franz Beckenbauer

———— ·•· ————

The last time Ireland played
England we beat them one–all.

Jim Sheridan in 1994

———— ·•· ————

They had a dozen corners,
maybe twelve, I'm guessing.

Craig Brown

Mirandinha will have more shots this afternoon than both sides put together.

Malcolm McDonald

Meade had a hat-trick. He scored two goals.

Richard Whitmore

If you had to name one person to
blame it would have to be the players.

Theo Foley

So that's 1–0. It sounds like
the score at Boundary Park,
where of course it's 2–1.

Jack Wainwright

The first ninety minutes of a football match are the most important.

Bobby Robson

Most football teams are temperamental. That's 90 per cent temper and 10 per cent mental.

Doug Plank

A BLOOD SPORT

I'm not happy with our tackling, boys. We keep hurting them, but they keep getting up.

Jimmy Murphy

If he fouls you he normally picks
you up, but the referee doesn't
see what he picks you up by.

Ryan Giggs on Dennis Wise

I'm always telling Craig Russell
to run at players with the ball,
and he does it. Do you know
why? Because I tell him I'll
break his legs if he doesn't.

Sunderland manager Mick Buxton

They say the new striker I'm
marking is fast. Maybe, but
how fast can he limp?

Mick McCarthy

❧

When David Webb was manager
of Bournemouth he never thought
training was any good unless
there'd been a punch-up.

Harry Redknapp

❧

The Liverpool theme song is
'You'll Never Walk Alone'.
The Wimbledon one is 'You'll
Never Walk Again'.

Tommy Docherty

Referees at Celtic–Rangers matches always have a hard time. One particular unfortunate, officiating at his first fixture, was checking in with the team managers before the kick-off. 'Well that seems to be everything,' said the Rangers boss, 'Now if you'd just like to give us the name and address of your next of kin, we can start the match.'

Edward Phillips

If his car broke down and I saw him thumbing a lift I wouldn't pick him up. I'd run him over.

Brian Clough on Peter Taylor following a row with him

It's not fair to say
that Lee Bowyer
is racist; he'd stamp
on anyone's head.

Rodney Marsh

Norman Hunter doesn't so much tackle players as break them down for re-sale as scrap.

Julie Welch

Get your retaliation in first.

Alastair Dunn

The rules of soccer are simple. If it moves, kick it. If it doesn't, kick it until it does.

Phil Woosnam

It's very unfair to ask any man
to stand in a human wall during a
soccer match. A high-speed leather
ball hitting you squarely in the
pleasure centre could raise your
voice by a hundred octaves and
have you talking like Quasimodo
for the rest of your life.

Pat Ingoldsby

In football it is widely acknowledged
that if both sides agree to
cheat, then cheating is fair.

C. B. Fry

TIME'S WINGED
CHARIOT

Chris Kirkland's
future is definitely
in front of him.

Andy Gray

He had an eternity to play that ball but he took too long over it.

Martin Tyler

As with every young player, he's only eighteen.

Alex Ferguson

Michael Owen isn't a natural goal-scorer yet. That takes time.

Glenn Hoddle

We're a young side that
will only get younger.

Paul Hart on Nottingham Forest

That youngster is playing well
beyond his nineteen years.
That's because he's 21.

David Begg

The ageless Dennis Wise,
now in his thirties.

Martin Tyler

My parents have been there for
me ever since I was about seven.

David Beckham

A SAFE PAIR OF HANDS?

You have to remember
that a goalkeeper is a
goalkeeper because
he can't play football.

Ruud Gullit

Neville Southall was a big daft goalie. He had a sponsored car but he couldn't drive. And he once turned up at Wembley wearing his suit and a pair of flip-flops.

Andy Gray

The Pope was a soccer goalkeeper in his youth. Even as a young man he tried to stop people from scoring.

Conan O'Brien

David Icke says he's here to save
the world. Well he saved bugger all
when he played in goal for Coventry.

Jasper Carrott

Dino Zoff is all right with the
high balls, but with the low ones
he goes down in instalments.

Ian St John on the former Italian keeper

He hasn't made any saves
you wouldn't have expected
him not to make.

Liam Brady

Dutch goalkeepers are protected
to a ridiculous extent. The
only time they're in danger of
physical contact is when they
go into a red-light district.

Brian Clough

Poor Scott Carson.
Just two more hands
and another chest and
he would have saved it.

Jimmy Greaves on one of the goals that
put England out of Euro 2008

That would have been a goal if
the goalkeeper hadn't saved it.

Kevin Keegan

—◆—

The most vulnerable area for
goalies is between their legs.

Andy Gray

—◆—

It's not nice going into the
supermarket and the woman at the
till is thinking, 'Dodgy keeper'.

David James

IDENTITY CRISES

Hoddle hasn't been the Hoddle we know, and neither has Robson.

Ron Greenwood

Who should be there at the far post
but yours truly, Alan Shearer.

Colin Hendry

There's no way Ryan Giggs
is another George Best.
He's another Ryan Giggs.

Denis Law

When it comes to the David Beckhams of the world, this guy's up there with Roberto Carlos.

Duncan McKenzie

If that lad makes a First Division footballer, my name is Mao Tse-tung.

Tommy Docherty on Dwight Yorke

The last player to score a hat-trick
in the FA Cup Final was Stan
Mortenson. He even had a final
named after him, the Matthews Final.

Laurie McMenemy

Duncan Ferguson became a legend
before he became a player.

Joe Royle

INTERNATIONAL DUTY

Other nations
have history. We
have football.

Uruguayan manager Ondino Viera

The Brazilians aren't as good as
they used to be, or as they are now.

Kenny Dalglish

———◆———

I'd love to play for one of those
Italian teams like Barcelona.

Mark Draper

If you have a fortnight's holiday
in Dublin you qualify to play
for the national side.

Mike England

—◆—

I've just named the team I would
like to represent Wales in the
next World Cup: Brazil.

Bobby Gould

The Croatians
don't play well
without the ball.

Barry Venison

The Koreans were quicker
in terms of speed.

Mark Lawrenson

The English football team
– brilliant on paper, shit on grass.

Arthur Smith

Playing with wingers is more effective
against European sides like Brazil
than English sides like Wales.

Ron Greenwood

———

To play Holland you have
to play the Dutch.

Ruud Gullit

———

San Marino play like men who
expect to encounter visa problems
if they approach the halfway line.

Tom Humphries

The tune began changing when
the Peruvians, a goal down,
suddenly revealed an ability to
run faster with the ball than the
Scots could run without it.

Clive James on the 1978 World Cup

When he came to the club, all he
could say in English was 'Yes', 'No'
and 'Morning'. A week later he'd
added 'Thank you' and 'Budweiser'.

Jim Duffy on his Czech signing, Dusan Vrto

Scotland has the only
football team in the world that
does a lap of disgrace.

Billy Connolly

———•———

I once attended a funeral on
the day Wales lost an important
match against England. It
totally spoiled the day for me.

Dai Jenkins

———•———

1966 was a great year for English
football. Eric Cantona was born.

Graffiti

SIX OF THE BEST

When they first
installed all-seater
stadiums everyone
predicted that
the fans wouldn't
stand for it.

George Best

I used to dream about taking the ball round the keeper, stopping it on the line and then getting down on my hands and knees and heading it into the net.

George Best

Bobby Collins was so small we used to say he was the only player in the league who had turn-ups on his shorts.

George Best

If Tommy Docherty says 'Good
morning' to you, check the weather.

George Best

When I see a group of men
walking towards me, it's always
a toss-up whether they're going
to ask me for my autograph
or smack me in the mouth.

George Best

Great managers have to be
ugly and swear a lot.

George Best

INJURY TIME

I was watching
Germany and I got
up to make a cup
of tea. I bumped
into the telly and
Klinsmann fell over.

Frank Skinner

Leeds United are having problems with injuries. The players keep recovering.

Bill Shankly at a time when Leeds were having a bad run

He's had two cruciates and a broken ankle. That's not easy. Every player attached to the club is praying the boy gets a break.

Alex Ferguson on Wes Brown

John Barnes's problem is that he gets injured appearing on *A Question of Sport*.

Tommy Docherty

Then there was the football fan
who sued a Scottish League
club because he was injured while
watching a match. He fell out of
the tree beside the grounds.

Jim McTaig

When England go to Turkey
there could be fatalities.
Or even worse, injuries.

Phil Neal

My ankle was pointing towards Hong Kong so I knew I was in trouble.

Manchester United striker Alan Smith
after breaking his leg in 2006

CLUB LIFE

The problems at
Wimbledon seem
to be that the club
has suffered a loss
of complacency.

Joe Kinnear

All Nottingham has is Robin
Hood. And he's dead.

Bryan Roy after he left Nottingham Forest

Robert Maxwell's just bought
Brighton and Hove Albion. He's
furious that it's only one club.

Tommy Docherty in 1988

As a small boy I was torn between two ambitions: to be a footballer or to run away and join a circus. At Partick Thistle I got to do both.

Alan Hansen

When I played with Barnsley it was a small-town club with a chip on its shoulder. Later I went to Millwall, a club with a chip on both shoulders.

Mick McCarthy

The two best clubs in
London are Stringfellows
and The Hippodrome.

Terry McDermott

❦

The last time Nottingham were
five points ahead of anybody
was in a cricket match.

Brian Clough referring to that team's
Premiership priority in 1977

❦

When you've been given a free
transfer by Rochdale you worry
seriously about your future.

Terry Dolan

Watching Manchester
City is probably
the best laxative
you can take.

Phil Neal

Southampton is a very well-
run football team from Monday
to Friday. It's Saturdays
we have a problem with.

Laurie McMenemy

Sheffield United couldn't hit
a cow's arse with a banjo.

Dave Bassett in 1994

Too big to be a wee club and too wee to be a big club.

John Rafferty on Clyde

When I was at St Mirren's, it was a desolate place. Even the birds woke up coughing.

Alex Ferguson

If Everton were playing down
at the bottom of my garden,
I'd draw the curtains.

Bill Shankly

❦

After I joined Celtic I was
walking down a street in Glasgow
when someone shouted 'Fenian
bastard'. I had to go and
look it up. Fenian, that is.

Mick McCarthy

BOTTLING IT

They say football
is a game of two
halves. Not for me
it isn't. I regularly
down eight or nine
pints while watching
a live game on Sky
TV in my local.

Adrian Bond

The Scottish football fan's ability
to smuggle drink into matches makes
Papillon look like an amateur.

Patrick Murray

The days of training on
Guinness are over.

Kevin Short

GEORGE BEST NEEDED FORTY PINTS

Unfortunately ambiguous newspaper headline
after Best received his liver transplant.
The reference is to blood, not beer

Kevin Keegan isn't fit to lace
George Best's... whiskeys.

John Roberts

It took a lot of bottle for
Tony Adams to own up
to his drink problem.

Ian Wright

I pissed it all up against a wall.

Brian Clough explaining how drink
ruined his managerial career

Alcoholism V Communism

Banner on display during the 1982 World
Cup when Scotland were playing Russia

The long ball down the middle is like pouring beer down the toilet. It cuts out the middle man.

Jack Charlton

❧

Let me recommend shopping to any young professional football player who feels they're in danger of going off the rails. It has less risk of personal injury than a punch-up outside a nightclub, and you very rarely end up with a hangover.

Brian McClair

CRYSTAL BALLS

The score is Ipswich
nil and Liverpool two.
If it stays that way,
you've got to fancy
Liverpool to win.

Peter Jones

The one thing I didn't expect
is the way we didn't play.

George Graham

The winner of the Premier League
will come from a select bunch of one.

Chelsea chief executive Peter Kenyon
as the 2006 season started

I don't think we'll go down. But then again, the captain of the *Titanic* said the same thing.

**Neville Southall on Everton's chances
of avoiding relegation**

We didn't underestimate them. They were just a lot better than we thought.

Bobby Robson

You've got to believe you're going to win and I believe that we'll win the World Cup until the final whistle blows and we're knocked out.

Peter Shilton

If history repeats itself I think we can expect the same thing again.

Terry Venables

LET ME
REPHRASE THAT

We spoke about it
for a while and out
of it came the fact
that he wouldn't
speak about it.

Terry Venables on a conversation he had
– or didn't have – with Middlesbrough
chairman Steve Gibson about his future

The secret of football is to equalise
before the opposition scores.

Danny Blanchflower

We're now going to Wembley for
live second half commentary on the
England–Scotland game – except
that it's at Hampden Park.

Eamon Andrews

The groin's a little sore but after the semi-final I put it to the back of my head.

Michael Hughes

The first half was end-to-end
stuff. The second half, in contrast,
was one end to the other.

Lou Macari

It was one of those goals
that's invariably a goal.

Denis Law

There are two ways of getting the ball. One way is from your own players, and that's the only way.

Terry Venables

I watched the game, and I saw an awful lot of it.

Andy Gray

It was a match that could have gone either way and very nearly did.

Jim Sherwin

Achilles tendons are a pain in the butt.

David O'Leary

There goes Juantorena down the back straight, opening his legs and showing his class.

David Coleman

He sliced the ball when
he had it on a plate.

Ron Atkinson

Is acne an occupational hazard for
football strikers, as in 'Duncan
Ferguson picked his spot
before tucking the ball away'?

Tom Shields

You can't take your eye off
this game without seeing
something happen!

Harry Gration

What I said to them at half-time
wouldn't be printable on the radio.

Gerry Francis

KISS AND TELL

Alan Shearer is so
dull he once made the
papers for having a
one-in-a-bed romp.

Nick Hancock

Is scoring a goal better than sex?
Well it's about five years since I did
either, so I must decline to answer
that question on grounds of amnesia.

Ken Cunningham

It's difficult to motivate players
if they earn forty grand a
week, have three Mercs, and
mistresses everywhere.

Joe Kinnear

If one of my girls walked in and said, 'Daddy, I'm going out with a footballer,' I'd say, 'No, you *were* going out with a footballer!'

Andy Gray

Football and sex are utterly different. One involves sensuality, passion, emotion, rushes of breathtaking ecstatic excitement followed by toe-curling orgasmic pleasure. The other is sex.

Joe O'Connor

When I was playing
for Manchester
United I used to
go missing a lot:
Miss America, Miss
Uruguay, Miss Peru...

George Best

A few more clean sheets and Sven's problems both on and off the field would disappear.

Brian O'Keeffe

If you gave me the choice of beating four men and smashing in a goal from 30 yards against Liverpool or going to bed with Miss World, it would be difficult to decide. Luckily I had both. It's just that you do one of these things in front of 50,000 people.

George Best

John Bond has blackened my name with his insinuations about the private lives of football managers. Both my wives are upset.

Malcolm Allison

I've been so wedded to Liverpool that I've taken the wife out only twice in forty years. It's time she saw more of my ugly old mug.

Bill Shankly after finally deciding to leave the club

STRATEGIC SKILLS

Fail to prepare,
prepare to fail.

Roy Keane

If there's an effective way to kill off the threat of Maradona by marking him, it probably involves putting a white cross over his heart and tethering him to a stake in front of a firing squad. Even then, there would be the fear that he might suddenly drop his shoulder and cause the riflemen to start shooting one another.

Hugh McIlvanney

———

There was no point in him coming to team talks. All I used to say was, 'Whenever possible, pass the ball to George.'

Sir Matt Busby on George Best

If one day the tacticians reached
perfection, the result would
be a nil-all draw... and there'd
be no one there to see it.

Patrick Crerand

The best way to deal with Ronaldo
is to stop the ball getting to
him in the first place. If it does
get to him, we have to make
sure he has no space to turn. If
that doesn't work, we'll have to
tie his shoelaces together.

John Collins on Scotland's World
Cup tie with Brazil in 1998

If all else fails, you could wait for the first corner kick and use his dreadlocks to tie him to the post.

Vinnie Jones on possible ways of dealing with Dutch ace Ruud Gullit in 1988

Ally MacLeod thinks tactics are a new kind of peppermint.

Simon Douglas

Football isn't just about playing well. It's about making the other team play not so well.

Roy Paul

If you played football
on a blackboard,
Don Howe would
win the World
Cup every time.

Willie Johnston

It's easy to beat Brazil. You just stop them getting within twenty yards from your goal.

Bobby Charlton

Anyone who uses the word 'quintessentially' in a half-time team talk is talking crap.

Mick McCarthy

APPEARANCE ISSUES

So that's what you
look like. I've played
against you three
times and all I've ever
seen is your arse.

Soccer international Graham Williams to
George Best after a bruising 1964 match

They're calling me Valdarama, but
I feel more like Val Doonican.

**Andy Townsend after dyeing his hair
blonde for the 1994 World Cup**

The image Mark Hughes conjures
up is one that makes a caricaturist's
pen convulse with joy: legs like
tree trunks, neck muscles that put
a pit bull terrier to shame, elbows
flailing in the penalty box and the
guts of a kamikaze bungee jumper.

Cefin Campbell

Ryan Giggs: the one with his eyes too close together, giving him the aspect of a village idiot.

Marian Keyes

Ian Rush's hooter is so big he should have 'Long Vehicle' stencilled on the back of his head.

Danny Baker

Kenny Dalglish wasn't
that big but he had a
huge arse that came
down below his knees.
That's where he got
his strength from.

Brian Clough

Bobby Robson's natural expression
is that of a man who fears he
might have left the gas on.

David Lacey

The last time I saw something
like that, it was crawling out of
Sigourney Weaver's stomach.

Ally McCoist on David Bowman of Dundee United

Mark Hughes is playing better
and better, even if he's going grey
and starting to look like a pigeon.

Gianluca Vialli in 1997

The person who said 'All men are created equal' never stepped into a footballers' changing room.

Eric Morecambe

How much further down his head will Bobby Charlton have to part his hair before he faces the fact that he's bald?

Clive James

THE LIFE OF BRIAN

I only ever hit Roy Keane once. He got up, so I couldn't have hit him very hard.

Brian Clough

I've seen big men hide in
corridors to avoid him.

Martin O'Neill on Brian Clough

A player can never feel too
sure of himself with Brian
Clough. That's his secret.

Archie Gemmill

We always discuss everything in
detail before deciding that I'm right.

Brian Clough on his locker room team talks

Very few players have the
courage of my convictions.

Brian Clough

WINNER TAKES ALL

Winning doesn't
really matter as
long as you win.

Vinnie Jones

Whoever wins today will win the championship no matter who wins.

Denis Law

I begrudge Manchester United their success, but I am not inconsistent. I begrudged them their failure too.

Tom Humphries

It's a no-win game for us, although I suppose we can win by winning.

Gary Doherty

Players win matches but
managers lose them.

Liam Harnan

We know what we need to do now
so I think we'll either win or lose.

Ian Rush

We got the winner three minutes
from time, but then they equalised.

Ian McNail

Winning isn't the end of the world.

David Pleat

———— ❧ ————

We lost because we didn't win.

Ronaldo

———— ❧ ————

For a few minutes it looked
like Wigan would win, but
then the game started.

Ken Ronan

IN A MANNER
OF SPEAKING

Not being in the
Rumbelows Cup
for these teams
won't mean a row
of beans, because
that's only small
potatoes to them.

Ian St John

Manchester United have got the
bull between their horns now.

Billy McNeill

Celtic have taken this game
by the scruff of the throat.

John Greig

Those are the sort of doors that get opened if you don't close them.

Terry Venables

And tonight we have the added ingredient of Kenny Dalglish not being here.

Martin Tyler

We can only come out
of this game with egg
on our faces, so it's
a real banana skin.

Ray Stewart before a crunch tie in
the Scottish Cup in 2001

Graeme Souness went behind my back right in front of my face.

Craig Bellamy

All that was missing was a wee rub of the green, when we went 2–nil down it was like shutting the gate after the horse had bolted. We left ourselves a mountain to climb.

Dunfermline boss Bert Paton after a defeat

We could be putting the
hammer in Luton's coffin.

Ray Wilkins

Sometimes you open your
mouth and it punches you
straight between the eyes.

Ian Rush

Liam Brady's been playing
inside Platini's shorts all night.

Jimmy Magee

If you don't like the heat in the dressing room, get out of the kitchen.

Terry Venables

For the benefit of Anglo-Saxon viewers, I wonder if the TV sports presenters would consider using subtitles when interviewing Kenny Dalglish.

Letter to the *Evening Standard*

GOD COMPLEXES

I wouldn't say I was
the best manager in
the business, but I
was in the top one.

Brian Clough

We're fourth in the table – fourth!
I'm going home to sit with a bottle
of Coke and a packet of crisps
and stare at the league table
on teletext for three hours.

Gordon Strachan

He likes publicity. He wears a card
around his neck saying, 'In case of
heart attack, call a press conference.'

Tommy Docherty on Manchester City
chairman Peter Swales in 1982

Jose Mourinho turned down the position of Pope when he heard it was only an assistant position.

Harry Pearson

Alex Ferguson's weakness is that he doesn't think he has any.

Arsene Wenger

The bottom line is that Beardsley is God.

Andy Roxburgh after Peter Beardsley scored Scotland's winning goal against England in 1988

GOALS, GOALS, GOALS

Norman Whiteside
was more a scorer of
great goals than a
great scorer of goals.

Paul McGrath

The best thing for them to do is stay
at nil–nil until they score a goal.

Martin O'Neill

I would have thought that the
knowledge that you are going
to be leapt on by half a dozen
congratulatory but sweaty team-
mates would be an inducement
NOT to score a goal at soccer.

Arthur Marshall

The twenty-first goal was offside.

Brian Keir after his Under-21 side
won a match by 22 goals to nil

Ryan Giggs did everything
there but score or pass.

Tom Tyrell

The fools. They've
scored too early.

Eamonn Sweeney on a 1998 game of Gaelic football
during which Sligo scored first and then lost

That's the kind of goal he
normally knocks in in his sleep
with his eyes closed.

Archie McPherson

Apart from their goals,
Norway haven't scored.

Terry Venables

It was the sort of
goal that made
your hair stand on
your shoulders.

Niall Quinn

Football is a funny game. Ron Davies scored 200 league goals in one season, but the last I heard of him he was working somewhere on a building site.

George Best in 1982

It was particularly pleasing that our goalscorers scored tonight.

Alex Ferguson

We were doing great before
they scored five freak goals.

Bert Head, former manager of Crystal Palace

Batista gets most of his
goals with the ball.

Ian St John

After I scored six against
Northampton I hung back for
the last part of the game. I
didn't want to score any more.
It was getting embarrassing.

George Best

Our problem is that we've tried
to score too many goals.

Gordon Lee

David Batty is quite prolific,
isn't he? He scores one goal a
season, regular as clockwork.

Kenny Dalglish

All strikers go through what they call
a glut when they don't score goals.

Mark Lawrenson

Woodcock would have scored there
but his shot was just too perfect.

Ron Atkinson

WAGS' TALES

Show me a man who loves football and nine times out of ten you'll be pointing at a really bad shag.

Jo Brand

The woman sits, getting colder
and colder, on a seat getting
harder and harder, watching oafs
getting muddier and muddier.

Virginia Graham

I'd rather have a guy take
me to a football match and
have a drink afterwards than
go to bed with someone.

Samantha Fox

I've read David's autobiography from cover to cover. It's got some nice pictures.

Victoria Beckham

When men are at a football stadium they're there to watch the game. You could prance half-naked across the pitch and the only response you'll get from the menfolk in the stalls is 'Get off'. Not, you'll notice, 'Get 'em off'.

Anne Marie Scanlon

I had no interest in going straight into football management after my playing career ended. My plan was to chill out for a few years and spend time with my family, but they got fed up with me. My wife dropped me off at the stadium.

Roy Keane

On the rare occasions he took me out, he talked about nothing but football. By the time I left him, I knew more about it than most managers.

Danielle Souness, the ex-wife of Graeme

A man's sexual
fantasy is two lesbians
and a donkey making
out to the music of
Match of the Day.
A woman's sexual
fantasy is a man
doing the hoovering
now and again.

Jo Brand

So Victoria Beckham got pregnant during the last World Cup. Well it's nice to see David had something on target.

Angela Miller

She Tarzan, he Jane.

Andrew Morton on the relationship between Posh and Becks

SURVIVAL OF
THE FITTEST

Ian Rush is perfectly
fit apart from his
physical fitness.

Mike England

He's put on weight and I've
lost it, and vice versa.

Ronnie Whelan

———

Damien Duff has been known
to suffer from Adhesive
Mattress Syndrome.

Brian Kerr

I've introduced something new to
the training. It's called running.

Gerry Francis after he took over as
manager of Spurs in 1994

Pat Crerand is deceptive:
he's slower than you think.

Bill Shankly

Pass a ball? He'd have trouble passing wind.

Alf Ramsey on Dutch international Piet Fransen

I had to remind the players that I've had open heart surgery and there's no way I can have this every week.

Graeme Souness after a 4–3 thriller between his Newcastle team and Manchester City in October 2004

UNSAVOURY
COMPARISONS

Vinnie Jones is to
fair football what
Count Dracula was
to blood transfusions.

Michael Herd

If you can imagine spending five
years with an overgrown child
clambering about in your attic
then you'll have a fair idea of the
impact Graeme Souness has
made on Scottish football.

Graham McColl

Steve Staunton's honeymoon
as manager of Ireland lasted
about as long as one of
Britney Spears' marriages.

Kevin Palmer

Kenny Dalglish was quiet in the Liverpool team talks until the players started talking about conditions. Then he came on like a Govan shipyard shop steward.

Graeme Souness

If you're a sports channel that doesn't have football, you're effectively shovelling water with a sieve.

Andy Gray

Listening to a modem starting up for ten minutes through a loud hailer would be soothing compared to having to endure one of Steve Staunton's press conferences. People have been known to get tinnitus of the eyes from reading his newspaper interviews.

David Kenny

What is it that Rangers, Celtic and a three-pin plug have in common? They're all completely useless in Europe.

Michael Munro

Trevor Ford used to collect
bookings like autographs.

John Charles

Comparing Gascoigne to
Pelé is like comparing Rolf
Harris to Rembrandt.

Rodney Marsh

Duncan MacKenzie is
like a beautiful motor car
– six owners, but he's been in
the garage most of the time.

John Toshack in 1978

Michael Owen used to be the baby-
faced assassin. Wayne Rooney is
more like the assassin-faced baby.

The Guardian

Trevor Brooking floats like a
butterfly – and stings like one as well.

Brian Clough

BORN TO LOSE

We've got a long
term plan at this club
and except for the
results it's going well.

Chairman of Fulham FC

In 1978, in between
Manchester City winning two
games in succession, there
had been three Popes.

Frank Skinner

A lot of hard work went
into this defeat.

Malcolm Allison

Where did it all go wrong for us?
It was quite simple really. At the
back, in midfield and up front.

George Graham after a 2–nil defeat
for Leeds by Aston Villa in 1996

We don't use a stop-watch to judge
our Golden Goal competition
now; we use a calendar.

Tommy Docherty on the standard
of play at Wolves in 1985

Those who tell you it's tough at the top have never been at the bottom.

Joe Harvey

—◆—

A robber recently broke into Sunderland's grounds and stole the entire contents of the trophy room. Police are looking for a man with a red and green carpet.

Michael Harkness

For years I thought the club's
name was Partick Thistle Nil.

Billy Connolly

My doctor told me I should
avoid any excitement so I've
started watching Millwall.

Les Dawson

The trouble with Freud is that
he never played the Glasgow
Empire on Saturday night after
Rangers and Celtic had both lost.

Ken Dodd

My local football team are so
bad, every time they get a corner
they do a lap of honour.

Bob Monkhouse

Some teams are so negative they
should be sponsored by Kodak.

Tommy Docherty

The FA Cup Final is a
great occasion, but only until
ten minutes to three o'clock.
That's when the players come
on and ruin the whole thing.

Danny Blanchflower

If I walked on water, my accusers
would say it is because I can't swim.

Former German coach Berti Vogts

QUICK ON THE UPTAKE

Velocity.

Kenny Dalglish as he dashed by a reporter who
had asked him for 'a quick word' after a match

When the TV people asked
me if I'd like to play a football
manager in a play, I asked how
long it would take. They told me
about ten days. 'That's about
par for the course,' I replied.

Tommy Docherty

❧

Verbal abuse.

Brian McClair after being asked what
he'd had free as a footballer

Ask any striker what was the greatest goal he ever scored and they'll all give you the same answer – the next one.

Ian Rush

Aye, Everton.

Bill Shankly to a barber who asked him if he wanted 'Anything off the top' in 1962

The gaffer said at the end of his team talk, 'Has anybody got any questions?' 'Yes,' I said, 'Where do babies come from?'

Brian McClair

Could I not have two bullets?

Alex Ferguson in October 2004 after being asked if he had a bullet in a gun, would he use it on Arsene Wenger or Victoria Beckham

The standard of
sweet trolleys at the
team get-togethers.

Pat Nevin after being asked what was the greatest
improvement in Scottish football in the past ten years

You say Tony Hateley's good in the air. Aye, but so was Douglas Bader – and he had two wooden legs.

Bill Shankly to Tommy Docherty

Fuck off Norway.

Paul Gascoigne to an Oslo TV crew in 1992
when they asked him for a pre-match comment
at Wembley before a World Cup qualifier

A chap was once trying to get me
to play for his club in America.
'We'll pay you $20,000 this year,'
he said, 'and $30,000 next year.'
'OK,' I replied, 'I'll sign next year.'

George Best

The first half was even. The
second half was even worse.

Pat Spillane

THE MONEY MEN

Kenny Dalglish calls his goals tap-ins until we come to the end of the season and we're talking money.

Bob Paisley

He's a money-grabbing cockroach.
I own two pot-bellied pigs and
they don't yelp as much as him.

Vinnie Jones after being sent off in February 1996
for fouling Ruud Gullit. He alleged Gullit 'dived'

Maradona was the highest-
paid handballer in history.

Con Houlihan

No wonder he met me at the
airport; the taxi fare would have
tipped the club into bankruptcy.

Niall Quinn on being picked up personally
by Fulham's manager Malcolm Macdonald
when he first signed for that club

Half a million for Remi Moses? You could get the original Moses for that, and the tablets as well.

Tommy Docherty

I get on a train and sit in second class
and people think, 'Tight bastard,
all the money he's got and he sits
in second class.' So I think, 'Fuck
them' and I go to first class. And
then they say, 'Look at that flash
fucking bastard in first class!'

Paul Gascoigne

They offered me a handshake
of £10,000 to settle amicably. I
told them they would have to be
a lot more amicable than that.

Tommy Docherty after being released
from Preston Football Club in 1981

My problem with Paul McGrath
was whether to give him appearance
money or disappearance money.

Ron Atkinson

The Sheffield United Board
have been honest with me.
When I came here they said
there would be no money and
they've kept their promise.

Dave Bassett

Premier League football is a multi-million pound industry with the aroma of a blocked toilet and the principles of a knocking shop.

Michael Parkinson

Tony Cascarino was the biggest waste of money since Madonna's father bought her a pair of pyjamas.

Gordon McLaren

A LITTLE BIT
OF IRELAND

The proliferation of
soccer in this island
is about the best
thing that happened
to us since the arrival
of the potato.

Con Houlihan

In the Dark Ages BC (Before Charlton) when we were crap, tickets for home games were as abundant on the streets of Dublin as nightclub vouchers midweek.

Conor O'Callaghan

Stephen Ireland is a riddle inside a mystery wrapped up in an enigma.

Garry Doyle after the soccer player withdrew from Ireland's World Cup squad in October 2007 due to personal problems

'You'll never beat the Irish' may have become one of football's eternal truths, but there's a very good chance that you're not going to lose to them either.

Paul Howard

———◆———

People think Ireland is divided into orange and green. Actually the predominant colour is red – Man United red.

Eamonn Holmes

A few of them moved faster than they ever did on the pitch!

Brian Kerr reminiscing about a night he spent in a Dublin Hotel in November 2003 when the Irish football squad were roused by a burglary and a bullet fired into the ceiling

Ever since Italia '90, every Irishman learned four words of Italian, '*Olé, olé, olé, olé*'. Except they were Spanish.

Niall Toibin

Jack Charlton's philosophy of soccer was, 'If plan A fails, try Plan A'.

Mark Lawrenson

Irish sides react as positively to the tag of favourites as a highly strung stallion does to first-time blinkers.

Robert Kitson

***

If Ireland finish with a draw in winning the game, that would be fine.

Jack Charlton

***

Danny Blanchflower was a lovely lad, even though he was Irish.

John Charles

Ray Treacy got 56 caps for Ireland,
and 30 of those were for his singing.

Eamon Dunphy

———

Most international studies of
human happiness show that the
average Irish person derives 63
per cent of his or her sense of
wellbeing from watching England
losing football matches.

Declan Lynch

AIMING BELOW
THE BELT

Wayne Rooney is
a potato-headed
granny-shagger.

Jonathan Ross

My second spell at Villa ended
in the summer of 1987 with the
arrival of Graham Taylor. You
could say it resulted from a clash of
personalities. I had one and he didn't.

Andy Gray

You should only say good
things when somebody leaves.
Robert has gone. Good.

Newcastle chairman Freddy Shepherd on Lauren
Robert after he left the club for Portsmouth

Who would have guessed that behind that arrogant Scots bastard image there lay an arrogant Scots bastard?

Mike Ticher on Tommy Docherty

———◆———

I call it *The Satanic Verses.*

Jason McAteer on Roy Keane's autobiography

Gordon Strachan's
tongue can kill a
man at ten paces.

Mick Henigan

I have never met Lee Bowyer,
but everyone I have spoken to
about him says he is a toerag.

Tony Cascarino

❧

Kenny Dalglish suffers from
constipation of the emotions.

Michael Parkinson

❧

I went to watch you once and
thought you were a fat, lazy bastard.

Jack Charlton to Tony Cascarino before
signing him to play for Ireland

When Frank Stapleton wakes up in
the morning he rushes to the mirror
and smiles, just to get it over with.

Tony Cascarino

Carlton Palmer covers every blade
of grass on the pitch – mainly
because his first touch is crap.

David Jones

If Osvaldo Ardilles had gone
to Arsenal, they'd have had him
marking the opposing keeper.

Danny Blanchflower

Eric Cantona couldn't
tackle a fish supper.

Alex Ferguson

He can't run, can't tackle and can't head a ball. The only time he goes forward is to toss the coin.

Tommy Docherty on Ray Wilkins

Beckham can't kick with his left foot. He doesn't score many goals. He can't head a ball and he can't tackle. Apart from that he's all right.

George Best

THE WORLD AT
THEIR FEET

I was both surprised
and delighted to
take the armband
for both legs.

Gary O'Neill

My knees are on their last legs.

Paul McGrath

＊

Most players would give their right arm for his left foot.

Mark Lawrenson on Jason Wilcox

＊

I wonder what would have happened if the shirt had been on the other foot.

Mike Walker

Ian Rush unleashed his left foot
and it hit the back of the net.

Mike England

My left foot is not one of my best.

Sammy McIlroy

Kevin Kilbane's head is better
than his feet. If only he had three
heads, one on the end of each leg.

Eamon Dunphy

David Seaman isn't great when he's
got to kick the ball with his feet.

Alan Hansen

I took a whack off my left ankle, but
something told me it was my right.

Lee Hendrie

———— ·•· ————

Being naturally right-footed,
he doesn't often chance his
arm with his left one.

Trevor Brooking

———— ·•· ————

He kicked wide of the goal
with great precision.

Des Lynam

MEA CULPA

People seem to think that Jack Charlton and myself were influenced by one another. Untrue. I was an arrogant bastard long before I got involved with him.

Mick McCarthy

If they'd used video evidence in
my day, I'd still be doing time.

Graeme Souness

———◆———

When I joined Rangers I immediately
established myself as third choice
left half. The two guys ahead of me
were an amputee and a Catholic.

Craig Brown

I daren't play in a five-a-side at
Anfield because if I collapsed no
one would give me the kiss of life.

Graeme Souness after open-heart surgery in 1993

We ended up playing football,
and that doesn't suit us.

Airdrie manager Alex Macdonald

The last time we played Seville
we were beaten 2–nil. And
we were lucky to get nil.

Nick McCarthy

One of the most difficult tasks I had
on match days was shaking hands
with the opposing manager if I'd lost.

Brian Clough

When we played football at school
I was usually put in goal – basically
because I filled most of it.

Janet Bryant

I promised I would take Rotherham
out of the First Division. I did
– into the Second Division.

Tommy Docherty

When I was admitted to the heart unit, somebody sent me a Get Well telegram that said, 'We didn't even know you had one'.

Brian Clough

One accusation you can't throw at me is that I've always done my best.

Alan Shearer

KEEPING UP
WITH JONES

Not only would I not
sign him, I wouldn't let
him into the ground.

Tommy Docherty on Vinnie Jones

I gave a little squeeze. Gently, of course. Gazza didn't squeal. Well, not a lot. I think he tried to but no sound came out.

Vinnie Jones on the (in)famous time he was photographed holding onto Paul Gascoigne's 'wotsits' during a match

Vinnie Jones is as discreet as a scream in a cathedral.

Frank McGhee

The Football Association
have given me a pat on the back
because I've taken violence off
the terraces and onto the pitch.

Vinnie Jones

Vinnie Jones has been sentenced
to 120 hours community service,
but this was reduced to 60 hours
on appeal – from the community.

Angus Deayton

If you're going to go over the top
on me you better put me out of the
game or I'll be coming back for you,
either in five minutes or next season.

Vinnie Jones

Vinnie Jones admits he threw a
piece of toast at Gary Lineker.
What he didn't say was that it
was in the toaster at the time.

Tony Banks

If you do that again I'll tear your
ear off and spit in the hole.

**Vinnie Jones to Kenny Dalglish
following a late tackle in 1987**

I always do that to people I like.

**Vinnie Jones after being asked why he bit a
journalist on the nose in a Dublin hotel**

MAKE YOUR MIND UP

Certain people
are for me, certain
people are pro me.

Terry Venables

When I said they'd scored two
goals what I meant, of course,
was that they only scored one.

George Hamilton

The game is finely balanced,
with Celtic well on top.

John Greig

We're on the crest of a slump.

Jack Charlton

Without picking out anyone
in particular, I thought Mark
Wright was tremendous.

Graeme Souness

For those of you watching
in black and white, Spurs
are in the all-yellow strip.

John Motson

The opening ceremony was
good, although I missed it.

Graeme La Saux

———•———

You can't guarantee anything
in football. All you can
guarantee is disappointment.

Graeme Souness

———•———

I'd rather play in front of a full
stadium than an empty crowd.

Johnny Giles

Our strategy is all-out attack
mixed with caution.

Jim McLaughlin

They're still in the game, and
they're trying to get back into it.

Jimmy Hill

I'm not a believer in luck, but
I do believe you need it.

Alan Ball

If Glenn Hoddle said one word
to his team at half-time, it was
concentration and focus.

Ron Atkinson

Everything in our favour
was against us.

Danny Blanchflower

DIFFICULT BODILY
MANOEUVRES

Martin O'Neill,
standing, hands on
hips, stroking his chin.

Mike Ingham

He caught that with the
outside of his instep.

George Hamilton

My legs sort of disappeared
from nowhere.

Chris Waddle

Once again it was Gough who
stood firm for Scotland in the air.

Jock Brown

241

With the very last
kick of the game,
MacDonald scored
with a header.

Allan Parry

We have to roll up our sleeves
and get our knees dirty.

Howard Wilkinson

I can count on the fingers of
one hand ten games where we've
caused our own downfall.

Joe Kinnear

In the last ten minutes of the match
I was breathing out of my arse.

Clinton Morrison

He shook hands with
us over the phone.

Alan Ball

Here at Old Trafford they reckon
Bestie had double-jointed ankles.

Alex Ferguson on George Best

Celtic manager Davie Hay has a
fresh pair of legs up his sleeve.

John Greig

I'd have to be deaf not to
read the allegations.

Bobby Downes

What he's got is legs, which the
other midfielders don't have.

Lennie Lawrence

That's not the type of header
you want to see your defender
make with his hand.

Ron Atkinson

PRESS GANGED

There's a place for the press but they haven't dug it yet.

Tommy Docherty

Attending a Kenny Dalglish press conference was akin to walking into a room in which a married couple have just had a major row about sex.

Harry Pearson

━━◆━━

I sometimes think I must be the only person in Britain who has featured on the front, centre and back pages of a daily newspaper – all on the same day.

George Best

I have told my players never
to believe what I say about
them in the papers.

Graham Taylor

———◆———

If Vinnie Jones hadn't existed, *The
Sun* would have invented him.

Dave Bassett

Mick McCarthy
breaks into a rash if
he's within thirty yards
of an NUJ card.

Tom Humphries on the former
Republic of Ireland manager

THE BOARDROOM
BOYS

John Cobbold's idea
of a boardroom crisis
was when they ran
short of white wine.

Bobby Robson on the former Ipswich chairman

I'm out at the moment, but should
you be the chairman of Barcelona,
AC Milan or Real Madrid,
I'll get straight back to you.

Answerphone message of Joe Kinnear

FIFA stands for Forget Irish
Football Altogether.

Mick McCarthy

If you dropped the FIFA crowd
into the ocean, they wouldn't be
able to decide if it was wet or not.

Jake Duncan

I'm drinking from a cup today.
I'd prefer a mug, but they're
all in the boardroom.

Tommy Docherty

When the FA get into their stride they make the Mafia look like kindergarten material.

Brian Clough

❦

The ideal board of directors should be made up of three men: two dead and one dying.

Tommy Docherty

❦

What would I do about football hooligans? Well, I'd start with the 92 club chairmen.

Brian Clough

www.summersdale.com